Angels
and Me

Carolyn Nystrom
ILLUSTRATED BY EIRA REEVES

Text © 1981 by The Moody Bible
Institute of Chicago
Design © 1993 Three's Company,
London

First published in this edition by
Moody Press in 1994
2nd printing 1996

ISBN: 0–8024–7863–8
Designed and created by
Three's Company, 12 Flitcroft Street,
London WC2H 8DJ
Worldwide co-edition organized and
produced by Angus Hudson Ltd,
Concorde House, Grenville Place,
London NW7 3SA

Printed in Singapore

Moody Press, a ministry of the Moody
Bible Institute, is designed for
education, evangelization, and
edification. If we may assist you in
knowing more about Christ and the
Christian life, please write us without
obligation: Moody Press, c/o MLM,
Chicago, Illinois, 60610.

Do you know about angels?
I do. Let me tell you.

God loves us so much that He takes care of us in ways we can't even see. Angels are one of these ways.

God created you and me and the earth and the stars — and angels. Thousands and thousands of angels.

3

Psalm 91:11

Angels have many jobs, but one of their special jobs is to watch over me — and you.

Usually we cannot see angels. They are invisible. But sometimes God gave His people special eyes so that they could have just a peek. Or sometimes God gave an angel a body like a person, so that the angel could do a certain job. Most of the time angels cannot be seen or heard. But we know they are still here.

Three angels looked just like men when they came to visit Abraham. Abraham and his wife were kind to them. They invited the three men to stay for dinner. Later they discovered the three men were angels with an important message from God.

Angels are very wise. They know more than you or I or even the wisest man on earth. But they do not know as much as God. God knows everything.

Psalm 103:20

Angels are strong — stronger than you or I or the strongest man on earth. But they are not as strong as God. God can do anything.

Angels can move fast — faster than the fastest airplane. They can be here one moment and far away in a second. But no angel can be in more than one place at a time. Only God can do that. God is everywhere — all the time.

9

What do angels look like? No one knows for sure. Artists have fun painting them many different ways — some with wings, some with white robes. They paint some to look strong, others to look gentle. They even paint some to look like babies. But these are all guesses about angels. The Bible doesn't tell us much about how angels look. Instead, the Bible tells us a lot about what angels do.

I wonder if God thinks what I do is more important than the way I look?

11

1 Thessalonians 4:16

The Bible tells us that there are several kinds of angels. Michael is an archangel. He fights against Satan. When Jesus comes back to earth to take His people to heaven the archangel, Michael, will come with Him. Won't that be exciting?

Isaiah 6:2, 6

Seraphim stand above the throne of God. They have six wings and can fly. They lead all of heaven in praise and worship of God. What do you think it will be like to praise God with the seraphim?

13

Genesis 3:24

Cherubim are magnificent creatures, hard to describe. They have many eyes and wings. Their job is to guard the holy places of God.

Angels

14

Exodus 3:2–5

One of the angels who visited Moses was called the Angel of the Lord. The Angel of the Lord came to people at a time when they had important decisions to make.

Angels do many kinds of work for God. They are God's messengers. Before the Bible was written, God often sent angels to give messages to His people.

Luke 1:35

When Jesus came as a baby, angels appeared often. They talked to Mary and Joseph, to the shepherds, and even to Jesus' uncle, Zacharias. The angels made sure that everyone in Jesus' new family was ready to take care of Him.

Genesis 19:12–13

Angels also carry out God's punishment. When people in Sodom became so wicked that they would never again turn to God, God sent angels to destroy them.

But I don't need to be afraid of angels because I belong to Jesus. God tells angels to take care of me. They can protect me from getting hurt. Even if things go wrong, the angels are still with me. That's their job.

When I gave my life to Jesus, Jesus was happy. And so was I. The angels in heaven saw it, and they were happy.

Now when I praise God, I can't hear the angels, but I know they are praising God too.

When I go to heaven to be with Jesus, then I will see the angels, and I won't have to imagine what they look like.

But I won't become an angel. God created me to be a person. And I will always be myself — even in heaven.

Matthew 24:31

Jesus will come back to earth with His angels. If I'm still here, Jesus will take me, and all others who believe in Him, home to heaven.

me

me

a baby angel

Then we will live forever in heaven with God and His angels.

Revelation 5:9–12

The angels will teach us to praise God. Together we will worship Him. But we will never, never worship the angels. They are not gods. God made them — just as He made us.

Will God let me see an angel before I go to heaven? Maybe.

28

But even if I never see an angel here, I can still thank God for them. Just knowing the angels are near helps me not to be afraid.

Angel
Book

Psalm 91:11–12 (*Today's English Version*)

God will put his angels in charge of you to protect you wherever you go. They will hold you up with their hands to keep you from hurting your feet on the stones.